Resell Rights Questions Answered

Jim Stephens

Published by RWG Publishing, 2021.

RESELL RIGHTS QUESTIONS ANSWERED

First edition. July 13, 2021.

Written by Jim Stephens.

Also by Jim Stephens

Kindle Publishing Made Easy: Autopilot Cash With Amazon Kindle!
Million-Dollar Secrets of the Amazon Associates: How They Make
Money From the Biggest Online Shopping Mall
Self-Publishing Made Easy: The Easy Way to Self-publish Your Own
Books!
Scam Busters: How to Avoid the Most Popular Scams of Today!
Affiliate Marketing and Blogging
The Quick and Easy Guide of Diamonds
Government Information
Hiking and Camping
Koi Pond
Law Information Guide
Motor Homes Research
Affiliate Marketing and Success Systems
Online Shopping
Outsourcing Ebooks and Software Jobs
Personal Loans
Resell Rights Questions Answered

Table of Contents

LEGAL NOTICE 1

Dear Aspiring Reseller, ... 3

Infamous Question #1: Are all Resell Rights products the same in terms and conditions? 5

Infamous Question #2: What is the difference between Resell Rights & Pvt. Label Rights? 7

Infamous Question #3: How do I compete with other Resellers who own the same product? 9

Infamous Question #4: What Ways Can I Profit from Resell Rights products? 11

Infamous Question #5: What Should I Look for in a Product before Purchasing Its Rights? 13

Infamous Question #6: Where are the Best Places to Search for Quality Products to Resell? 15

Infamous Question #7: How do I market a Resell Rights product? 17

Reseller Tips: How to Compete with Other Resellers in the Marketplace 19

LEGAL NOTICE

Dear Aspiring Reseller,

———

Dear Aspiring Reseller,
Exchange Rights can sound all "outsider" to you particularly in the event that you are new to the showcasing scene or essentially stepped in straight from the universe of working together traditionally.

Maybe you are more acquainted with the expression "retail" and "discount" in the disconnected universe of working together yet a few things can change somewhat in the realm of E-Commerce however many have named Internet Marketing as a method of selling through the Internet as a medium with a large number of the traditional and dependable standards unblemished.

So at this point that you've caught wind of Resell Rights, you're likely considering what is the issue here and how you get your own slice of the pie from it. I was the point at which I previously found the might of Resell Rights.

More or less, most top advertisers today support their pay and add spikes to their traffic and edges to building their mailing records through imaginative use and influence on Resell Rights. What's more, it can possibly be your influence to your next leap forward in Internet Marketing, as well, however just on the off chance that you comprehend it first !

Believe it or not. So on the off chance that you have questions like beneath, overflowing and beating hard in your mind right, this book is for you.

• What is Resell Rights?

• Why are there an assortment of terms in Resell Rights and what are the distinctions?

• How would I take advantage of this worthwhile chance in the E-Commerce scene and tie along with my next Information item?

• And whatever other inquiries that most starting advertisers and rookies have on the unique subject of Resell Rights wealth!

Having exchanged a few items all through my Internet Marketing profession, I have been frequently posed inquiries, some of them remembered for the above notice, on this one of a kind field. So beneficial but risks are that you don't discuss this with your neighbor-nearby except if the person is an Internet Marketer.

Having said that, on the off chance that you need to realize how to bring in cash from Resell Rights items you need to comprehend it first, right? What's more, to comprehend a subject you don't know by any means, you must ask a specialist regarding the matter, right?

All things considered, here it is – the scoop from the Master Reseller for all yearning affiliates: the 7 scandalous Resell Rights questions replied.

In this book, I've arranged seven of the most well known inquiries posed on benefitting from Resell Rights, particularly since I saw they will in general be repeating questions. Furthermore, it is conceivable you have a few or these inquiries to you standing by to be offered an explanation to fulfill your inquisitive brain.

So turn the page and remember to send me a card to say thanks when you make your first buck in the Resell Rights field. You know the location!

Infamous Question #1:
Are all Resell Rights products the same in terms and conditions?

Answer:

All Resell Rights are not made similarly. Exchange Rights fluctuate starting with one item then onto the next, with various rights, terms, and conditions. Indeed, a few items that are contained in a Resell Rights bundle are not for exchange by any stretch of the imagination, however are rather for individual utilize as it were.

In the event that you buy an exchange rights bundle, which contains more than one item, the bundle will commonly contain an exchange permit arrangement for every item. Try not to expect anything! Peruse each expression of the exchange permit before you exchange the item, and save that permit in a protected spot for future reference.

For certain items, you might be permitted to exchange the item at any cost, or even part with it for nothing. Others may have a set value, implying that you can't sell the item for not exactly that cost or part with it free of charge. On account of actual items, like CD's or DVD's, you could conceivably be permitted to copy the item when you sell it. A few organizations may expect you to buy the item straightforwardly from them for exchange – for every deal.

There are normally different agreements for exchanging an item too, other than the cost at which you may exchange it. For example, most item creators will have severe enemy of spam strategies, implying that the item can't be publicized by any technique that might be infringing upon government spam laws.

In the event that you are ever uncertain about your exchange rights, contact the creator of the item prior to doing whatever else. You would prefer not to disregard any terms or conditions, as it can and will be viewed as an infringement of intellectual property laws, which is a government offense. Ensure that you're not simply asking another affiliate – contact the creator of the item straightforwardly.

Ensure that you don't lose your licenses. Print them out and keep them on a document. You should likewise back up electronic duplicates on a circle. Incorporate any email trades with the item creator also in your reinforcement documents, including the messages that you send.

Infamous Question #2:
What is the difference between Resell Rights & Pvt. Label Rights?

A nswer:

Numerous individuals are befuddled about the distinction between exchange rights and private name rights. A few erroneously imagine that they are exactly the same thing, and this isn't so. It is simple, be that as it may, to see how the two terms can be befuddling.

On the off chance that you have exchange rights, you reserve the privilege to exchange the item, related to the agreements set out in your permit, with no guarantees. This implies that you can't modify or alter the item in any capacity, and you can't put your name on it as the creator.

On the off chance that you have private name rights, nonetheless, you can alter constantly the item as you see fit, and you can even put your own name, or your organization's name, on the item as the creator. You can change words, sections, illustrations, add to the item, separate the item into a few unique items – whatever you decide to do.

Since you have more opportunity with private name rights, these sorts of items for the most part cost more to buy the rights for. A few items even have two alternatives when you buy them: exchange rights or private name rights. Indeed, you can utilize your private name rights items and sell the exchange rights to other people, after you have changed the item and put your name on it.

There is additionally a distinction between exchange rights and expert exchange rights. Exchange rights basically give you the option to exchange the item, while ace exchange rights permit you to exchange the item and the exchange rights!

Once more, it is not difficult to perceive how one could be mistaken for these different terms. Be that as it may, whenever given the decision, consistently go for the private name rights. This will permit you to have your very own result, without really making one yourself. Most private mark rights licenses give you substantially more tolerance.

Infamous Question #3:
How do I compete with other Resellers who own the same product?

———

A nswer:

Numerous individuals keep away from exchange rights items basically on the grounds that they accept that they can't rival other affiliates who are selling a similar item, or they feel the market for that item might be overflowed because of the way that there are an extraordinary number of other affiliates.

Notwithstanding, all things being equal, a great many people buy exchange rights, and have no aim of exchanging the item – they essentially needed the item. Others buy exchange rights to sell the item, yet genuinely don't have a clue how, or don't utilize exceptionally powerful promoting methods. Truth be told, 90% individuals who hold the equivalent exchange rights that you hold are treating it terribly.

You should likewise think about the market. While it is more diligently to sell Internet Marketing related items, selling non-Internet Marketing items is simpler than you might suspect. The explanation it is more enthusiastically to sell Internet Marketing items is on the grounds that the greater part of the other affiliates will truth be told be Internet Marketers who do understand what they are doing.

To begin with, you should expand your promoting endeavors. By accomplishing more, you will put yourself well in front of the 10% that are really promoting the item effectively. Discover new business sectors for the item and better approaches to contact them.

Consider holding teleseminars or joint wandering with different advertisers who have enormous supporter records.

Then, make your bundle more appealing than other people's. You commonly won't reserve the option to change the item, however that doesn't mean you can't change the offer. Utilize different items as rewards, as long as you reserve the option to part with those items. Meat up your bundle, and you will pull in front of the opposition rapidly. Additionally, change your direct mail advertisement. Try not to utilize similar direct mail advertisement that other affiliates are utilizing. Make yours extraordinary.

Infamous Question #4:
What Ways Can I Profit from Resell Rights products?

———

A nswer:

There are numerous approaches to benefit from exchange rights items. The primary way, obviously, is to just exchange the item. Notwithstanding, there are ways that you can understand much more benefits. It's anything but somewhat thought and imagination.

At the point when you sell the item, have an extra item or items to sell as an upsell or backend item. For example, sell the exchange item at 39.95, then, at that point have an upsell, or a connected item, that you offer either on your request page at an expanded cost, for example, 49.95 or 59.95. Your upsell could even be a participation site, for which you would gather month to month enrollment charges from your clients.

You can likewise publicize a backend item on the thank you page. This is an item that is offered after the acquisition of the first item is made, at an alternate cost. Backend items can cost more than the first item, the equivalent, or even less.

You can likewise benefit more from your exchange rights items by repackaging it, including more items, and raising the worth of the bundle – which thus raises the cost. On the off chance that you have ace exchange privileges of the item, which permits you to sell the exchange rights also, you can make a decent bundle of different related items and sell exchange rights to that bundle too.

You could even basically sell the item, or part with it in the event that you are permitted to do as such, to utilize a crush page to gather quality leads. A huge rundown of value drives opens numerous beneficial entryways. For example, you could go into joint endeavor arrangements to offer high ticket items to your rundown, or lease your rundown out to different organizations for a charge.

Nonetheless, before you begin utilizing different techniques for expanding your benefits with exchange rights items, it is vital that you read your permit consent to be sure that you are not infringing upon any of the terms.

Infamous Question #5:
What Should I Look for in a Product before Purchasing Its Rights?

Answer:

Before you buy exchange rights, you need to do some exploration to discover

regardless of whether buying the exchange rights will be beneficial for you. Not all exchange rights items merit having.

To begin with, investigate the actual item. Is it a quality item? Despite the fact that your name isn't on the actual item, your name will be related with selling the item, and you would prefer not to sell garbage. Along these lines, ensure that the item does what it guarantees, and that it is to be sure of worth.

Then, you need to investigate the market. Is there a business opportunity for the item? A simple method to discover is to do a hunt in Google utilizing catchphrases that potential clients would use to look for the item. Take a gander at the locales that are promoting comparative items.

The supported advertisements are the ones you are keen on. Individuals and organizations don't persistently go through cash publicizing items that are not selling. On the off chance that cash is being spent on promoting, there is a business opportunity for the item. Additionally take a gander at related magazines to check whether cash is being spent on promoting.

Peruse the permit arrangement prior to making the buy. In the event that it's anything but accessible to you without buying first, leave. You need to check the permit to ensure that you can showcase the item successfully, utilizing techniques that you know work.

You need to know whether the direct mail advertisement changes over, however you additionally might need to ensure that you are permitted to change the direct mail advertisement as you see fit.

Additionally check whether you can discover the number of individuals are as of now exchanging the item. Is the market overflowed? Recollect that 90% individuals with exchange rights either will not be exchanging the item, or they don't have a clue how to adequately advertise the item.

After you've taken a gander at all of these issues, and addressed these inquiries, you will know if you should buy the exchange rights item. In the event that the item has benefit potential, it merits purchasing.

Infamous Question #6:
Where are the Best Places to Search for Quality Products to Resell?

———

Answer:
With such countless items with exchange rights available, it's difficult to pick which ones merit the expense. There are, in any case, approaches to discover quality items to sell, on the off chance that you realize where and what to look like.

To start with, search for items that don't have exchange rights. These will normally be the most beneficial, if there is a business opportunity for the item and you realize how to showcase it, basically in light of the fact that there are no exchange rights advertised. The thought is to contact the item creator and request restrictive exchange rights to the item.

Some item creators will say no, and some will not react by any stretch of the imagination – yet when an item creator does react and says yes to your offer, you may have discovered a goldmine. Settle on sure that you get the understanding recorded as a hard copy and endorsed before you begin promoting the item.

Another incredible method to discover quality items to exchange is to join quality exchange rights participation locales, for example, the Internet Marketing Profit Center at http://InternetMarketingProfitCenter.com. You need participation to destinations that make the actual items, or have the items made only for them, instead of exchange rights locales that just sell you exchange rights bundles that they have purchased from different sources.

Some exchange rights participation destinations, like ResellRightsMastery, have items made only for their individuals and offer exchange rights bundles that were not made only for them, and this is an optimal site. This permits you to discover items that are not flooding the market, too as items that can be utilized as upsells and backends for one another.

On the off chance that you are buying exchange rights for items that you just go over that offer such rights, make sure to do your exploration first – prior to making the buy. Ensure that there is a market. Peruse the permit consent to ensure that you can advertise the item successfully. Ensure that you look at the item to guarantee that you will offer your current or potential clients a quality item too.

Infamous Question #7:
How do I market a Resell Rights product?

———

Answer:

Exchange rights items offer you the capacity to sell your own item, without really making one. While this gets you past one obstacle – the formation of an item – you actually have another obstacle to confront. How would you showcase an exchange rights item?

The first and most ideal choice is to advertise the item to your mailing list. On the off chance that you don't have a mailing list, construct one. There are different approaches to do this, yet the speediest method to assemble a rundown is to offer a free item, which is promoted with pay-per-click or through other people"s records. At the point when the possibility shows up at the site to accept their unconditional present, they should fill in their name and email address, and allow you to email them later on.

Pay-Per-Click publicizing can be utilized for more than list building, in any case. You can likewise utilize pay-per-snap to advertise your exchange rights item. Google AdWords is outstanding amongst other compensation per-click programs in presence today, yet there are numerous different alternatives, including Yahoo Search Marketing.

You can likewise buy publicizing in related bulletins, which are additionally called ezines. This is a compelling method to showcase an item, and it's anything but a proven strategy. You can discover quality bulletins by doing look in the ezine catalogs on the web.

Article showcasing is additionally exceptionally compelling. You basically compose articles that identify with your item, or have them composed for you, and submit them to the different article banks, permitting others to understand them and use them for content for their bulletins and sites, free of charge. At the lower part of your articles, add an asset box, which is basically a about the writer' section, which ought to incorporate a connection to your business page.

You can likewise joint endeavor with individuals who have enormous mailing records. Simply ensure that their rundowns are comprised of individuals who will be keen on your item. It doesn't bode well to showcase football items to a mailing list that is generally comprised of ladies who are keen on plans.

Reseller Tips:
How to Compete with Other Resellers in the Marketplace

———

H ow might you rival other affiliates who are selling precisely the same item at precisely the same cost to precisely the same market? It's really simpler than you may might suspect!

To begin with, recall that 90% surprisingly who hold the equivalent exchange rights permit that you hold either will not advertise the item by any means, or will not showcase it effectively. This basically implies that just 10% of the individuals who have exchange rights to a similar item are in contest with you. In any case, it truly doesn't make any difference how cutthroat the market is or the number of other affiliates there are for a similar item. At the point in the end, the solitary thing that truly tallies is the manner by which the item is showcased – how it is introduced to the market.

The primary thing you should do is separate yourself from the pack. Try not to worry about the thing others are doing. Do whatever you might feel like doing. Do what works. Start by making the item as various as your permit will permit you to. Change the bundle to incorporate rewards that others are not advertising. Additionally change the direct mail advertisement. Make it totally extraordinary, and more compelling than it as of now is.

Whenever you've changed the item and the bundle however much you are permitted to, the time has come to perceive what others are doing, to a degree. For example, on the off chance that you intend to showcase utilizing Google AdWords, see what watchwords your rivals (other affiliates) are offering on, and what they are paying. Either pay more, or bid on various, more designated watchwords.

For instance, on the off chance that you are selling a data item on weight reduction, don't utilize weight reduction as your watchword, or some other normal catchphrases. All things considered, use weight reduction for men, or weight reduction for ladies more than 40. Limited your market however much you can. You can wager that most of your rivals won't utilize such consideration in picking watchwords!

Likewise utilize different strategies for advertising the item. Market to your email list. Market to others' email records. Compose articles and appropriate them to the article banks. Hold teleseminars. The significant thing is to set up yourself as a specialist in the field that is identified with your item, and put yourself aside.

Don't miss out!

Visit the website below and you can sign up to receive emails whenever Jim Stephens publishes a new book. There's no charge and no obligation.

https://books2read.com/r/B-A-VNEK-YFKQB

BOOKS 2 READ

Connecting independent readers to independent writers.

Also by Jim Stephens

Kindle Publishing Made Easy: Autopilot Cash With Amazon Kindle!
Million-Dollar Secrets of the Amazon Associates: How They Make Money From the Biggest Online Shopping Mall
Self-Publishing Made Easy: The Easy Way to Self-publish Your Own Books!
Scam Busters: How to Avoid the Most Popular Scams of Today!
Affiliate Marketing and Blogging
The Quick and Easy Guide of Diamonds
Government Information
Hiking and Camping
Koi Pond
Law Information Guide
Motor Homes Research
Affiliate Marketing and Success Systems
Online Shopping
Outsourcing Ebooks and Software Jobs
Personal Loans
Resell Rights Questions Answered

About the Publisher

Accepting manuscripts in the most categories. We love to help people get their words available to the world.

Revival Waves of Glory focus is to provide more options to be published. We do traditional paperbacks, hardcovers, audio books and ebooks all over the world. A traditional royalty-based publisher that offers self-publishing options, Revival Waves provides a very author friendly and transparent publishing process, with President Bill Vincent involved in the full process of your book. Send us your manuscript and we will contact you as soon as possible.

Contact: Bill Vincent at rwgpublishing@yahoo.com www.rwgpublishing.com